Black's Young Naturalist's Series

BIRDS OF BRITAIN

WILD DUCK

BLACK'S YOUNG NATURALIST'S SERIES

BIRDS OF BRITAIN

BY

WILFRED WILLETT

WITH EIGHT PLATES IN COLOUR
SIXTEEN FROM PHOTOGRAPHS AND
DRAWINGS IN THE TEXT

LONDON
ADAM AND CHARLES BLACK

FIRST PUBLISHED 1950
BY A. & C. BLACK LTD
4, 5 AND 6 SOHO SQUARE LONDON W.1

To

ELIZABETH, MICHAEL AND MARK

MADE AND PRINTED IN GREAT BRITAIN BY
MORRISON AND GIBB LIMITED, LONDON AND EDINBURGH

CONTENTS

ILLUSTRATIONS

These eight plates are in colour.

CHAPTER I

ABOUT BIRD WATCHING

SOME trees, like oaks, shed their leaves in the autumn and remain naked all the winter. Others, like the pines, keep their needle-like leaves and only change the old ones for new leaves after several years. And in winter, instead of flowers we see berries, such as the bright red holly berries. And there is wet ploughland or green winter corn like grass where in summer the tall wheat stood. So the country in winter looks very different from what it will look like in spring and summer.

There are as many changes in the bird world, too, between winter and summer and spring and autumn. Some birds, like the Robin and Thrush, we always have with us wherever there are parks and gardens. Swallows and the Cuckoo, and many others, we only see in the warmer months of the year. But two kinds of Thrushes, the field-fare and the redwing, come to this country to spend the winter here. And then many Gulls, Ducks and Plovers come to us. Many birds live in different places in winter and summer and feed on different food. For instance, thousands of Black Headed Gulls fly about the Thames Embankment, the river and the London parks in winter and are glad to swoop on any scraps of food waste thrown to them ; but most of them go away in the spring. Birds change their feathers usually once a year at mid-summer or soon after, discarding the old worn-out feathers for new ones in moulting. These new feathers may not at first be very bright, for we would expect to see new feathers as smart as new clothes. But every new feather nearly is a little longer than the old one, which makes their " coats " thicker for the winter. Just as our clothes become shiny and thinner after wearing them, so also do the feathers of a bird wear a little during the winter. The tips of the feathers wear off (it is called " abrade ") and show the bright spring colours that we look for when the cherry trees are flowering and there are primrose clumps on the hedge banks. In some kinds of birds the tips of the new feathers may be a different colour and so make the colour of the bird different in autumn and winter from what we look for in the spring. I have just told you that thousands of Black Headed Gulls come to London and other towns in winter, yet these Gulls have white heads with a couple of small dark spots. It will be only when the white tips of their chocolate head feathers are worn away that they will be " black-headed " gulls. And if you look closely you will see that the colour is chocolate and not black after all. So not only have we to expect many different kinds of birds as the seasons of the year come and go, but also the birds change their plumage which may completely alter their appearance. In most kinds of birds their colour will only look duller in winter.

There are also many kinds of birds in which the male or cock bird has a different appearance and colour from the female or hen. The cock Blackbird is a glossy black bird with an orange bill whereas the hen Blackbird is a brown bird with a mottled breast. The cock Chaffinch is gaily coloured, the hen is the sober olive and brown. You can think of many examples, the duck and drake, the cock Pheasant and the quiet brown hen, the House Sparrow, the Bullfinch, the Hawks, and many others where the cock and hen have differently coloured plumage. It is the hen that lays the eggs and in some kinds of birds she does most of the hatching and rearing too. It is therefore useful for her to have sober coloured plumage that blends with her surroundings when she is sitting on the nest. But it makes it harder to identify some birds unless you find pleasure in quietly watching them and getting to know them as a family. Where birds live and what they do, when they sing and when they scold, and in fact their comings and goings throughout the year.

So now we know that not only do we have to expect to see the same bird sometimes in different places according to the time of year, but also to see it sometimes in quite a different dress. It makes bird identification more exciting. If all birds came and perched on the bush in front of us like the Robins do I think we should get bored with bird watching. As it is we never know what birds we may see. And we have usually to be quick to use our eyes otherwise the bird will have flown.

Very soon after you have taken to bird watching as your hobby you will begin to realise that you can distinguish them " a mile off," because they do things in a way peculiar to themselves ; for instance, a Song Thrush cocking his head when he is feeding on the lawn or meadow, the switchback flight of the Green Woodpecker, the hovering of a Kestrel above the field, a Tree Creeper running up the trunk of a tree like a little mouse, the Tits swinging upside down on a twig, and many more you will get to know as you watch birds. Then there is their calls, their flight call that some birds utter while they are flying, their cry when they are angry or frightened, and their song which is mostly heard in the nesting season. Everything like this is going to help you.

Most birds get their own food. (A few, like the Skuas which are northern sea birds, habitu-ally rob others of what they have gathered.) And many of them have developed particular kinds of bills most suitable for getting their food : the House Sparrow is a corn eater and so he has a strong large bill compared to the Hedge Sparrow who eats small insects and weed seeds. The Ducks have a shovel ; the Heron and King-fisher a dagger to spear and capture fish ; the Woodpeckers a bradawl which they drive into the wood to get at wood-boring insects. Then again the place where a bird usually lives to get

its food often makes a great difference in its
shape and appearance : a Swift, which spends
its day flying high in the sky, getting flies and
gnats, has very long wings but its four tiny
toes point to the front so that it clings to ledges
and cannot perch upright as a Robin does ;
on land, Ducks waddle because their bodies are
long and their feet are rather far back, but in
the water they ride like a boat, and swim easily.
Some diving birds have their legs and feet so
far back that they walk with their breast on the
ground and use their wings to help them.
Penguins cannot fly but their wings are used as
fins when swimming under water to catch fish.
Many of the birds that feed on soft mud or sand
have long legs and long bills like the Curlew
and the Snipe. And the long legs of the Heron
enable the bird to walk in water when it searches
for fish. Then the perching birds, like the
Thrushes, have three toes in front and one at the
back, so they grasp whatever they are perching on
rather like we grasp a branch when climbing a
tree—if we, for the sake of the example, think
of our thumb as the bird's hind toe. But if
the bird had to use its muscles to cling on to its
perch all night, it would either not get much
sleep or it would fall off when it was fast asleep,
dreaming it was flying. That does not happen,
because when the bird settles down, with its
breast on the perch, the legs are bent. This
tightens the toe muscles and tendons so that the
grasp of the perch will continue tight till the
bird wakes and stands up.

Ducks and Gulls do not sleep on perches or scratch for their food : they have webbed feet and sleep on the water or just settle down on the bank or shore. Not all water birds have their toes joined by a web : the Coot and Grebes have peculiar lobes on their toes : and some birds, like the Ringed Plover, can swim, if it has to, though it has no webs or lobes at all on the toes. The Plover has not even got a hind toe, so you would know it was not a perching bird. Some water birds, particularly those that chase fish under water, like the Cormorant and the Gannet, have their hind toe turned to the front and joined to the other toes with a web. These birds have to swim very quickly under the water to catch the fish on which they live.

Woodpeckers have another kind of foot. They climb up tree trunks as easily as a fly does on the wall. But many tree trunks have rough ridged bark which the Woodpecker is able to grasp with his feet the more easily because he has two toes turned behind and two in front. As well as his toes the Woodpecker has a stumpy tail which is pushed against the bark to help steady himself.

Notice accurately everything you can about the bird you are watching. It is these little things that give you a clue to what its name is. The size of the bird is important. And the best way to judge that is to compare its size with a bird you know, or better still, one that you see at the same time. Have a pocket-book—the cheaper the better—and make truly accurate notes of the bird you are watching at the time.

If your notebook is cheap you will not mind it getting a few raindrops on it. Don't try and look the bird up in a bird book then and there, for your notes will be much better if they are what you have seen without prompting from a book. Hurried reading may lead you to think the bird is something different from what it really is. If you note everything you can accurately, then you will be able to hunt it out in your bird book in the evening. If you are still puzzled ask in your local museum, or failing that ask at your local library if they would put you in touch with a local bird expert. Not many of us are artists, but try and get into the way of making drawings of the bird and its actions. It does not matter how rough they are as long as the drawing is as accurate as you can make it. Soon you will surprise yourself with how much of the character of the bird is in your rapid sketch.

The following is a rough guide of what you should note :

1. Date.
2. Place.
3. Time.
4. Size.
5. Shape (sketch).
6. Size, shape and colour of bill, legs and feet.
7. Size, shape and colour of tail and wings, with precise position and colour of bars or markings.
8. Colour and marking of rump.
9. What doing and how, when feeding, resting, flying.
10. Colours and markings seen in flight, on the ground.
11. Calls or song.
12. Exactly where bird was and how many there were.
13. Weather and wind.

You may think all this is making a lot of trouble when you only wanted to watch birds. If you will begin your bird notebooks early you will find you get great pleasure out of them. There is a saying that beginners have all the luck, and it may happen to you that you will see some rare bird which only carefully taken notes at the time will prove the fact. But whether you have such luck or not, you will find your knowledge of birds growing as your notebooks increase in number. Number the pages and index your notes. Some people copy out their notes in the evening into a loose-leaved notebook : in this way you can keep all your notes on a particular bird together, but that is only one of many ways. The important thing is to index your notes so that you can find your way about them easily.

As soon as you can, borrow or try to get someone to give you a pair of binoculars, or if that is too expensive get a telescope. That is the only thing that costs money in bird watching, but once you have a pair of binoculars they will last you many years with care. Don't take them to pieces or ever clean them as that will probably ruin them. It is better to take them back to the makers. With your glasses you can tramp the winter shore, daring the gale and the snow to get near to flocks of wild birds like the old shore gunners did. You can walk by the summer stream, or through the wood in springtime when the warm air is vibrating with the gentle notes of newly arrived summer birds. On moors, cliffs, lakes, you will find in each place new and exciting birds to you. And take a companion with you on your " bird walks," for two pairs of eyes are better than one pair and often one sees what the other would miss. Besides, most people find enjoyment is increased when you can share it with others. Only be careful to speak quietly if a bird is near. If you want to draw your companion's attention, whistle softly and nod towards it without otherwise moving. If you speak and point the bird would probably take fright and fly away.

In the following chapters you will find that most of the birds described are nearly always to be seen at the time and place mentioned. If they are not one day they will usually be there the next. They are called " The Common Birds." They make up the majority of our bird population without which our country would not be the pleasant place it often is. Because they are common birds we must not despise them, for after all we ourselves are " The Common People." Learn to know them, as that is the foundation upon which all our knowledge of them is built. And there are quite a lot of things of one kind or another that the experts still want to know about some of our common birds.

for if so the bird may desert it. Just glance in as you pass by. One day you will see a white, brown-spotted egg lying in the hair-lined cup. Next day another, and so on till there are usually five. By that time the hen is sitting very close. The cock does not usually help in hatching. In a fortnight the eggs hatch and then both parents feed the young. Another fortnight and they will be ready to fly. They have no red breast yet, but only brown mottled ones : the red breast will come with their summer moult. If you want to have really valuable notes, which will be worth much more than reading up what other people write without trying to check it from your own observation, you should make notes of the dates of these happenings. When did the young open their eyes ? When did the first feather sheaths show ? What food did the parents bring, and how often ? Perhaps you will not be able to note all the information in one year, but if you are careful with your notes, putting down all you see and not what you are in doubt about without marking your doubts in some way, you will be able to add to your knowledge in subsequent years.

The Song Thrush is another bird which we see on garden lawns, on the grass near shrubberies in parks, and even sometimes on the cricket pitch and football fields. Fortunately they are very common, for they have a lovely song that you hear on mild days throughout the winter, and in spring days when the first of the year's flowers are blossoming under the pussy willows their

SONG THRUSH WITH NEST AND YOUNG

Plate 2

H. Marcus Stone

Plate 3   MISTLE THRUSH AT NEST

song comes strong and clear over the countryside from the tall tree or bush. It is after an April shower when the sunbeams are sparkling on the young grass that a Song Thrush is sure to come down to the short grass to seek for worms and insects. He is greyish-brown on the back, but his speckled breast is the thing you notice most, and that he is much bigger and a different shape from the Robin. And a Song Thrush feeds in a different manner, too. He runs a few yards quickly, then stands very still while he looks about him. Suddenly he bends forward and cocks his head on one side, just as though he was listening to two worms gossiping. Actually he is not listening but looking. For Thrushes and most birds have their eyes one on each side of their heads, like we have our ears, with the result that they can see nearly all round them all the time and therefore are less likely to be taken by surprise and have no time to fly away. We use both our eyes to focus on one object and cannot use them to see different things like the Thrush does. So our Thrush on the lawn saw a movement, focused one eye on it, waiting for the worm to put his head out again, and then pounced and quickly dragged him out of his hole to eat.

If this Song Thrush is a cock you will see him in the evening perching on the fringe of small branches half-way up a hedgerow tree and singing his lovely song which he often begins with notes that seem to say " Pretty Dick, Pretty Dick, Pretty Dick " before going in to his warble. The hen Thrush will be busy with her nest. It tree, and you often hear the cock singing high in the tree during a winter storm.

These two Thrushes and the Blackbird we see winter and summer, though you may find their numbers change with the change of season if you keep count as you should do. But two other Thrushes come here in the winter—the Redwing and Fieldfare. They are usually seen in open country and fields, though in severe weather they are seen in town parks. The Ring Ouzel, which is a moorland bird with white breast band and which behaves rather like the Blackbird, leaves this country at the end of the summer. Watch for these birds and note when they come and, if possible, when and where, or in what direction, they go.

There are two more birds that are common in gardens and parks—the Hedge Sparrow and the House Sparrow. Although they are both called Sparrows these two birds belong to different bird families and live very different sort of lives. Try and compare them as soon as you have a chance. The House Sparrows are brownish in colour and the cocks have black bibs. You usually see them in small flocks of a dozen or so birds, hopping perkily about on the street or the garden. When disturbed they fly up to perch on the hedge or window-sill nearby and chirp noisily to one another as though protesting. The Hedge Sparrow on the other hand feeds alone, or occasionally with his mate, in the shadow of the hedge and disappears into it as soon as you approach without any fuss or noise. The House Sparrow

BLACKBIRDS

Male (centre) Female (right) Young (left)

Plate 4

GREAT TIT AT NEST HOLE

Plate 5

H. Marcus Stone

Plate 6   BLUE TIT

have no connection with coal. There is another Tit you may see on the fat, especially if the weather is frosty with snow on the ground, that is the Marsh Tit. They, too, go about in pairs, and go searching about old tree stumps, the ground and low stems for insects. They do not come into gardens very often, preferring to keep to the woods and coppices. You will have no difficulty in recognising them for they have a very glossy black cap and are brown on the back.

To see the fifth Tit, the Long Tailed Tit, you will have to walk in the country, across the fields and along the wood's edge. There, in the slanting beams of the winter sun, the hedgerow and the wood are many coloured on the frosty day. Then flitting down the hedge comes a flock of thirty or more Long Tailed Tits, often with other Tits and little birds. They swing on the twigs and fly on again past their fellows to settle again and search for insects. They have a tiny body, a black-and-white head and a tail that seems three times as long as the body. You cannot mistake them for any other bird you are likely to see. In the spring the flock will break up and each pair will build a lovely roofed nest decorated outside with lichens woven with cobwebs while inside are pushed sometimes thousands of feathers. The nest is built in a hedge or bush and is placed about five feet from the ground. You will find it more exciting watching and guarding it than trying to get an egg out of it. You will see the hen sitting, to hatch the eggs, looking out of the entrance with the end of her

tail showing over her head.   And then when the
eggs hatch there will be the growing young, watching for their parents to come with insect food.
At last, if you are lucky, you may see them leave
the nest : they come out one after another till you
can't imagine how they all could have grown up
in there.   It is a good thing that there are so
many, because, when the winter is severe with
long hard frost, these little birds often die from
cold and lack of food.

It is quite easy to persuade the Great Tit and
the Blue Tit to nest in a garden where they have
come for scraps and fat in the winter.   Get some
1-inch board, 5 inches wide.   Saw off a 9-inch
length and three 10-inch lengths.   Drill a hole
$1\frac{1}{2}$ inches in diameter and $1\frac{1}{2}$ inches down from
one end of the 9 inches.   Stand the 9-inch piece,
with the hole in the upper half, with two of the
10 inches behind flush with each edge, at the
back of the bench and nail together.   Then turn
it round and nail the other 10-inch piece and you
have now the four sides of the nest-box.   Nail a
piece of wood flush at the bottom, like a box, and
saw the top of each side diagonally so that you
can fit a sloping roof on without having a gap
in the front.   The roof should lap over the front
a little like house roofs do.   This you can fix on
with a hinge, but I nail mine.   To fix it, screw in
two screw eyelets and then you can either wire
or screw the nest-box wherever you wish ; but
be sure it does not get the blaze of the midday
sun as young birds cannot stand great heat.   I
do nothing else to my nest-boxes and some have

been occupied every spring for over a dozen years. I find about six feet from the ground the best height for these two Tits, and you will find it more interesting to fix nest-boxes so that you can see at least one from your window. Then you will see a pair taking grass and moss to line the nest, then ten days of inactivity while the eggs are being hatched, then a busy fortnight, when the parents come every two or three minutes of the day with bills loaded with caterpillars. I think, calculating from my observations, that the parents bring a thousand caterpillars and insects a day when the young are getting fledged.

If you are lucky enough to have a big garden you can make larger nest-boxes and place them higher in trees with the hope of enticing Woodpeckers, Nuthatches and Owls to nest in them.

GREEN WOODPECKER

CHAPTER 4

SWALLOWS

IF we walk through the young corn by the field
path at Whitsun we shall see our first Swallows
of the year. They fly swiftly, low, almost
touching the lush green blades, darting and turn-
ing with easy strokes of their pointed blue wings
in tireless flight after gnats and flies. Probably
these Swallows will go on farther north before
they come to their nesting places. The first
birds to reach our southern shores do so early in
April and even in March if the weather is spring-
like. And if there is no return of winter, more
and more will come nearly every day, to spread
over the country till in May they reach Scotland.
There will be still some newcomers to our shores
all throughout May, but the main rush of them
comes about the time we hear the Cuckoo's first
clear notes and know that spring has come.

There are three other birds that people often
call " Swallows." They are the House Martin,
the Sand Martin and the Swift. It is quite easy
to tell them apart as they fly. And all of them
spend most of their day in the air because their
only food is insects they take on the wing, and so
we must be able to tell which of the Swallows
it is as they glide around so smoothly and so
delightfully.

H. Marcus Stone

Plate 7　　　　MARSH TIT (page 29)

A Swallow has a dark-blue back and wings ; in fact he has no white at all on his back and only a few white spots on his tail that you probably will not see in the flying bird. The House Martin, however, has a showy white rump. This white patch on their back you cannot help seeing every time a House Martin turns in his flight or stops fluttering his wings for a moment as he snaps up a fat fly. You very seldom see Swallows do that. They fly swiftly all the time, skimming the tops of the corn or flicking a wing-tip into the surface of the river as they flit along in the evening calm. So low do they usually fly that you can see down on their blue backs and see they have no white on them. But you probably see their graceful forked tails, each fork tapering to a single, long slender feather called the streamer. The House Martin's tail is forked, but has not got these long streamers. House Martins, too, are white underneath from chin to tail. The Swallows have a chestnut throat and often the white underneath is tinged with chestnut.

Swallows are birds of the marshes, the river and the lakes. They build their nests of straw and mud on the top side of rafters in the stable and other farm buildings, in boathouses and now even on the steel beams of iron garages. The Swallows like to live where they have plenty of water handy and vast open spaces where they can fly at speed for a mile or more without hindrance of trees and buildings. The House Martins are not so particular. They will nest on marsh farmsteads, but they are just as much at home where the fields are bounded by hedges in which there are great oaks. Then you see the difference of flight. The House Martins circle round the field, very often at nearly tree-top height, and not at the speed of the Swallow although their flight is swallow-like. It is the House Martins that build their nests under the cottage eaves. The birds make neat clay balls by getting little blobs of mud and mixing it with their saliva, which makes the mud like cement when it dries. The birds line the nest with feathers. If not disturbed, House Martins will return year after year, repairing the nest more efficiently than many a house and cottage is repaired these days.

Too often it happens that the House Sparrows, instead of troubling to build their own untidy-looking nests, pop in and finding a good draught-proof Martin's nest begin filling it with hay for their own use. Then when the Martins return they find their nest occupied by squatters. There is no housing shortage for the Sparrows and so no excuse for squatting. There is often a heap of hay in the stackyard with which they should have built their own nest in the ivy. There are stories that House Martins have revenged themselves by sealing up the nest entrance with mud. No one has ever seen this happen. The Sparrow is too strong and cheeky a bird to let this happen, and it is always the Martins that go and build elsewhere.

There is another swallow-like bird that you see flying high in the air, not only above the tree

tops but often much higher than any church
steeple. Along they go, perhaps five or six
against the bright evening clouds, with their long
narrow wings curved like a bow and their bodies
making the arrow. They use these wings with
quick, stiff beats, then glide and tilt over sometimes one way and sometimes the other and the
wings beat again. These birds are Swifts. You
see them flying high in the air above towns as
well as villages and the countryside. They look
quite black when you see them against the sky,
but when they swoop from on high right
down to the few inches of a stream you will see
that they are really sooty brown in colour without
any white to be seen in their plumage. Swifts
seem to dive like this mostly in May and early
June. You can hear the swishing sound as they
hurtle by and you wonder how it is that they
pull out of their dive and glide and fly up again.
I have never seen two birds collide, but a friend
of mine once did so. He was driving along a
country road when two swifts collided and one
dropped into a turnip field while the other flew
on. He got out and searched for it and at last
found the Swift dead with its head injured.

Swifts build their nests usually in crevices under
the eaves and in holes in a thatched roof, or in
broken brickwork. They also nest in slits and
holes of cliffs, just as they used to before men
built houses. Like Martins and Swallows they
use saliva to glue into a cup-nest whatever they
can pick up in the air, straws blown by the wind,
feathers, seeds and anything light. Swifts have

very long wings, for they spend most of their time in the air. Therefore they cannot go and pick up whatever they want to build their nest like the garden birds do, because Swifts cannot run about as their wings would trail on the ground and their legs are short and weak. That is why you see Swifts diving so low in May and June, for it is then they are getting materials to build their nests. I have never seen Swifts on the ground, but some people have occasionally. You do see them clinging to a ledge near the nest quite often if you know where they are nesting.

Swifts are the last of the Swallows to come here in the spring, and are seldom seen before May even in the southern counties. And they are the first to go. Above my Kentish village during August I shall see them flying in family parties all the day and well into the twilight. Then one day before the end of the month all of them will go. Sometimes I see a few in September flying to the south-west, but they never loiter to weave in and out of the high air for insects. You should know that Swifts are not really in the same family as Swallows. Only near relations.

There is one other Swallow, the Sand Martin. This is the smallest of the four Swallows we have in this country. It is also the one that is seen least unless you live where there is a colony. For they live in colonies, each pair burrowing a small tunnel about a yard into the sand-pit face, or sometimes a river bank or a cliff. The end of the tunnel is made a little larger and there the birds bring bits of straw and some feathers to make a nest for the four or five white eggs which a hen Sand Martin lays.

They are noticeably smaller than the other Swallows and are brown on the back and not blue like the House Martin and Swallow. Besides the differences of size and colour, Sand Martins have a brown breast-band below the white throat. Otherwise they are white beneath. Like Swallows they like to be near water. I have seen thousands of them flying a few inches above the ebbing tide on a sandy shore in the late afternoons of September—flying sometimes between children paddling, and I have paddled out and watched them just skimming the little waves. The birds had gathered from many colonies and perhaps they would turn out to sea soon or else roost for the night in some reed bed.

For all the Swallows are migrants. I have just told you that you can see Sand Martins migrating in September along the seashore. You can often see them flying like this on inland lakes and rivers. And in September, if you get up as early as the workers on the farms, you will see the telephone wires sagging with the weight of thousands of Swallows and House Martins, perching wing to wing. The sun shines forth clear of the eastern wood, and all the gossamers and spiders' webs on the stubble, the stack, and the hedges shine with tiny rainbows as the sun-beams slant on the dew-drops. The birds begin to twitter and at last leave the wires and begin hawking after insects for their breakfast. Actually, all the Swallows, Martins, and Swifts have to go on catching insects all the day, from dawn till dusk, in order to get enough food not only to nourish but to give the energy to fly so fast and so long. And when they have young in the nest they must catch enough insects to keep themselves fit and to feed their growing youngsters for about three weeks. Even for a short time after the young have left the nest you will often see their parents giving them mouthfuls on the cowshed roof.

SWALLOW FEEDING YOUNG

CHAPTER 5

SUMMER BIRDS OF OUR LANE

Two hundred years ago we had very little farm-
land in this country and very few roads. There
were not in the whole of England then nearly
so many people as live in London to-day. And
most of the people lived in the villages and grew
what food they wanted. They made many
things—ploughs and carts, cottages and shelters,
beds and tables. But this isolated life in villages
was a hard struggle. After the English Revolution
things began to change. The land became the
property of rich farmers who grew much more
than the little villagers could. New machines,
new crops and better animals made it possible
to feed the rapidly increasing town population.
Many villagers went to work in the town and
found their lives even harder.

These changes must have affected many of
our birds too. Much scrub and woodland were
made into fields, hedges were planted, barns and
sheds were built, and the lanes were used. The
numbers of small birds increased, finding a home
in the hedge. But the Kite, Raven and the
Hawks decreased as man advanced his fields
into the wilderness that these birds thought their
own.

The main road as we see it to-day did not

exist fifty years ago. A main road now is not usually a good place for birds, in fact many birds shun it. But the winding, narrow lane always has plenty of flowers and birds. Lanes where there are trees and banks, and where the tall hedges comb hay out of passing farm waggons. There in April and May you hear the songs of many warblers newly come from Africa. The male birds come first, as a rule, and the hens about a week afterwards. They seem to come rather suddenly. There is an April shower and then bright sunbeams shine on primroses and violets sparkling with raindrops. Suddenly a little slender bird whispers a sweet song. It is rather plaintive as though asking you to be kind to it. Another also begins to sing a little way up the lane. You peer into a hazel bush in the hedge and see the slender bird is not at all concerned about asking favours of you. It is much too busy searching the young leaves and picking off what must be very small insects and caterpillars. Every now and then he whispers his sweet song as he is searching for his food. He has a thin bill and he is greenish-brown, very slim and only half the size of a Robin. This is a Willow Warbler or Willow Wren and one of the commonest Warblers.

There are lots of other Warblers, as this bird family is called. They all, except the rare Dartford Warbler, come to us in the spring, sing and nest, and then fly to North Africa and other places for the winter. All Warblers are slim birds that spend most of their time in trees and

Plate 9   CUCKOOS (*page 45*)
Adult (below)   Young (above)

bushes, searching for insects and caterpillars. And they sometimes eat berried fruit, like currants, raspberries, and take a peck at a cherry. Their slender bodies are well suited for slipping in and out among leaves as no Robin or Thrush could do. For these two get most of their food from the ground and often have a tug-of-war with a worm. Warblers' bills are fine and slender, and are just the right instrument for picking off tiny insects from delicate leaves.

The Willow Wren you should notice had brown legs. For there is another bird on a tree branch, which you might have thought was another Willow Wren. It is quite a job to tell them apart except for two things. This bird has black legs and in a minute it will sing " chiff-chaff, chiff-chaff, chiff-chaff." And that is its name, Chiff-Chaff. The song is softer than the " teacher, teacher, teacher " of the Great Tit. The Chiff-Chaff and the Willow Wren are called " leaf warblers " because they are so often seen picking off insects from leaves. There is another leaf warbler, the Wood Warbler or Wood Wren. It is seen mostly in woods searching the young leaves of trees. It is a little bigger and yellower than the Willow Wren, and has a pretty song which it sings usually at the top of the tree.

In a clump of brambles and fast-growing nettles there is another Warbler. He keeps down out of sight, creeping about this tangle of vegetation. When he does appear for a moment you see he is a browny-coloured bird with a grey cap and a white throat. He is called a Whitethroat. Country children called the bird the " nettle creeper " because it is so often seen creeping about the nettles by the hedge. The hen bird has a brown cap which is not very noticeable as a cap because the whole back plumage is brown. But you can tell the White-throats are Warblers by their actions, their bills, and their slim bodies.

You may see the Lesser Whitethroat. This bird is a much greyer bird and has more white on its throat. The hen is grey too. Although it creeps about thick tangles of old grass and brambles, the Lesser Whitethroat does pop up into the trees sometimes. I often see one during the summer in my apple trees, searching for insects. But if you go near the nest when the young are in it the Lesser Whitethroat comes up and from a low perch scolds so harshly and loudly you can hardly believe such a noise could come from so small a bird. The other Whitethroat will scold too, but not quite so noisily. Neither bird has much of a song, but you should be able to recognise these apart after watching them singing a few times.

As you walk on down the lane in May you will hear Thrushes and Blackbirds singing. They are familiar songs to you. Now you hear a song nearly as loud and beautiful, but quite a different tune. It comes out from a small oak tree in a sunny stretch of the lane. You get closer, trying not to be seen. At last you are near enough to see a lovely grey bird with a showy

black cap. And that is its name, Blackcap.
Although it is about the length of the House
Sparrow, it is slim and has a thin bill and so
you know it is a Warbler. The hen Blackcap
is easily distinguished as she has a distinct brown
cap. She is browner than her mate, but as both
birds come fairly frequently into the open on to
trees you will get to know them quicker than
the Whitethroats.

Because of the difference of plumage between
the male and female Blackcap, it is easy to tell
that the male birds come first to your district
when you are staying in the country. I always
hear one singing before I realise the Blackcaps
are arrived. I believe they sing at frequent
intervals and if the bird finds a desirable
territory that is his way of telling other cocks
he has occupied it. His song may be also to
advertise for a mate. In a few days if the
weather is sunny the hens arrive. Then, sad
to relate if you have thought the cock's song
was his way of showing his love and joy, most
good observers are convinced that once the hen
arrives the Blackcap's song deteriorates. See if
you think this is so.

There is another Warbler, the Garden Warbler,
that you may see in a wooded lane—in fact,
there is slightly more chance of seeing it than
the Blackcap. Their song is similar and you
have to have a good ear and be a good observer
before you can say which bird it is, a Garden
Warbler or a Blackcap. But once you can see
the bird there is no difficulty. The Garden

Warbler is a brown bird, buff coloured underneath, and is plumper than the Blackcap. These two Warblers are the best singers amongst the summer migrants and this is a help in their identification from the other Warblers.

In many country lanes the Nightingale can be heard. Everyone wants to hear a Nightingale sing because they have read so much about what a wonderful song it is. But most people have never heard it, except on the radio. The reason for this tells you some facts about the Nightingale. Firstly, he only sings for about six weeks in the latter end of April and during May—a time when few people are on holidays. Secondly, Nightingales are practically only found in the south-east of the country and do not go much north of the line stretching from Exeter to the Wash. And thirdly, they sing in the day and unless you know their song you may not distinguish it from that of the many other bird songs. For Nightingales, like other birds and we human beings, vary in their singing powers. One bird will be a star performer, while the next one however hard he tries will never be able to put up anything but a second-rate performance. And whatever the poets may have written, it is the male Nightingale that sings.

Because Nightingales are migrants and come here in April and sing, you must not think they belong to the Warbler family. They are nearer the Robin family and they look like a rather large brown Robin. They feed much on the ground, just as Robins do, and are plump in shape and not slender like the foliage flitting Warblers. Their nest, too, although built low down in undergrowth by the hedge or in the plantation like most of the Warbler's nests is built on a foundation of dry brown leaves just as the Robins build. And when the young first fly they are spotted, which is again like young Robins. If you want to find a Nightingale try and mark the place early in May where you hear him singing at night and when most of the other birds are asleep. Then go to the place after breakfast, though before is better, and you will probably hear him still singing and be able to spot him in a bush. A Nightingale is not so constantly on the move like the Warblers are. And you can make a lot of notes on him for your notebook. Don't forget it is May the Nightingale sings, and he stops very early in June when he is busy helping his mate to feed the young.

The Cuckoo has been calling, and now it flies across the field and perches in a laneside tree. It is a grey bird, with long pointed wings and a long tail. It looks rather like a grey hawk, but its flight is leisurely with its wings moving only a little up and down at each beat. The bird calls " cuckoo " as it flies and again several times from the tree. The Cuckoo is a migrant, coming to us in April. The males come first. The females follow in about ten days. Although the females do " cuckoo " sometimes, their call is a lovely sound like bubbling waters. Instead of building her own nest, the hen Cuckoo lays her eggs in nests of small birds, such as the Meadow Pipit and Hedge Sparrow. She watches them building and then lays one of her eggs when she is ready. She only lays one egg in a nest, so she has to find about a dozen nests of the kind of bird she victimises. For one hen Cuckoo nearly always uses only one kind of small bird to bring up her young. She doesn't look into a nest and then decides what colour egg to lay. That would be impossible. The parent Cuckoos leave this country at the end of June, but young Cuckoos do not leave till the end of August or even later. Soon after the young Cuckoo hatches from the egg, it pushes the other young out of the nest. Thus it grows quickly and has all the food the foster parents bring.

Our Cuckoo is a parasite, but it is a useful bird, feeding on many harmful caterpillars. Other Cuckoos in other parts of the world make their own nests. And do you know that there are lots of wild " cuckoo " bees ?

LAPWING IN FLIGHT

Plate 10 MAGPIES

CHAPTER 6

BIRDS OF THE MEADOW

Most people call Rooks " Crows." We say " As
the crow flies." We use a crow-bar. We find
crow-berries and crow-foot buttercups. And
there are many more examples. I think this
confusion about Rooks and Crows is because
most people are content to call any large black
bird a Crow without really looking at the bird.
We have one kind of Rook but two kinds of
Crow. One, the Grey Crow, has a grey mantle,
and the other is black like the Rook. The black
Crow is called the Carrion Crow. The grey
Crow is the Hooded Crow.

Rooks are birds of the fields and are mostly
seen in flocks. They nest together in a rookery
at the top of tall trees. In the winter they fly
in a long line straight over the country to their
roost. They go in a leisurely way every afternoon
on the same invisible broad highway. You can
follow them up and find where they roost. It
will take you a few afternoons as you can't go
across country " as the crow flies." You see
them tumbling and sliding about the air, cawing
and chuckling especially in the autumn, in fact
it seems as though they were playing games with
each other. The Carrion Crow on the other hand
usually keeps to himself or goes about in pairs,

47

flying more sedately and not so high up as the rooks.

But the best way to tell them apart is to look at their faces. The fully grown Rook is " clean-shaven " and you see the bare skin on the cheeks and chin. The Crow has black feathers and bristles right up to his black bill. Young Rooks, however, have very nearly fully feathered faces. Then you have to rely on the difference in flight, the fact that the flanks of a Rook look more ragged, and the Rook's plumage has more violet in it and the Crow's more green. The bare face of a Rook is as much a part of the bird's character as is the red breast of a Robin. The feathers are not " worn down " as used to be thought.

Jackdaws are also black birds. You cannot mistake them for Rooks if you are careful, for Jackdaws are smaller and have rather silvery heads except in front. They also move more quickly on the ground and their wings beat obviously faster, as you see when Rooks and Jackdaws fly up out of the field as they often do. Although Jackdaws like to nest in old towers and cliffs, they are very sociable and often flock together with Rooks in the fields.

In Kent, where I live, and in many other counties too, you often see two or three black-and-white birds in a field. They are about the size of a Pigeon, but with a much longer tail. These are Magpies. And they are the easiest birds to recognise at once, both on the ground or flying. Watch them hopping about carrying their tails well up, sometimes walking, and then

SWIFT *(page 35)*

Plate 11

H. *Marcus Stone*

Plate 12   GREAT SPOTTED WOODPECKER
(*page 14*)

as they see you they fly off over the trees looking
rather like giant tadpoles. If the light is right
behind you, and you are near, you will see what
appeared black is a blue or green velvet colour.
You sometimes hear it said that so-and-so
" chatters like a Magpie." As you hear the real
Magpies chattering stridently to one another in
the trees, you will hear them making a noise as if
every bird was shouting what he thinks, and does
not care what his neighbour has to say. Sometimes you see twenty or thirty Magpies in a field,
perhaps you will come upon them when the birds
are holding a " Marriage " display about Christ-
mas time. No one knows quite what it is all about
so make very careful notes of all you see. There
may be more than a hundred birds there together.
The Magpie's nest is large and stuck near the
top of a bush or hedge for all to see. It is built
of sticks and is roofed, too, with them

Even more gregarious than Rooks are Starlings,
if one takes the size of the flocks for comparison.
And the word " gregarious " only comes from
the Latin word meaning flock. In large fields
you very often see hundreds of Starlings, mingling
with the flocks of other birds, such as Lapwings,
Golden Plovers, Thrushes and Rooks. They do
not feed in a bunch as some other birds do,
but each Starling is quickly walking about busily
pecking here and there whenever he finds some
insect or seed. Sometimes he may use his bill
to track down an insect in the grass. He is
about the size of the Song Thrush of our gardens,
though less graceful in outline. His breast is

dark shining green, which in the distance may look black, and is covered with light buff spots. In fact, the Starling is speckled nearly all over in the winter, but less so in spring. In the autumn great flocks of Starlings come to us from Denmark and Holland and countries nearby. So there are many more Starlings here in the winter than in summer. The flock instinct is most in evidence when Starlings go to roost for the night. Little flocks and big flocks fly in from their feeding grounds, ten miles away, and often from greater distances. This roost may be in the reed beds of lakes and rivers, a wood, or buildings in towns. The flocks join up, and then many thousands of starlings will fly round, split up into two flocks, wheel round and join up again. These manœuvres go on for about an hour against the sunset clouds. You need not go out of London to see the Starling flocks flying round the roost at sunset, for they roost in great numbers on the buildings around Trafalgar Square. I believe they also roost on the City Buildings in Birmingham. When you watch the Starlings flying you will see they look like a shower of black arrows because of their short tails and short, pointed wings, and as they often glide in flight this arrow effect seems more striking

The roost breaks up in the spring and pairs of Starlings seek out holes in roofs and trees wherein to nest. Sometimes they nest in colonies. Young Starlings are mouse-coloured till the winter. The outline and behaviour of Starlings are so definite and distinct that you should not find it difficult to be certain what they are wherever you see them.

The Lapwing is another bird that you should soon get to know at sight, for it, too, has actions and an outline that at once distinguish it from other birds. It nests in the cornfields, meadows and marshes, and sometimes even on the moors and downs. In the spring you see a pair of Lapwings tumbling about in the air on very rounded wings, calling " Pee-wit " so loudly that you can hear it two fields away. They twist and turn, rising a little and then again tumble until they are a few yards from the ground when they straighten out and climb for another display. There may be more than one pair in a large field, especially near the marshes. Lapwings look bigger than Pigeons, and have longer legs and neck. But the first thing that strikes one is the crest towards the back of the head. It is in the winter you should get to know Lapwings. Then they will be in flocks on the ploughland and the winter corn, on the new ley grass springing up in the stubble fields and on the low-lying meadows. There they stand, perhaps a hundred or more seemingly black-and-white birds, sometimes taking a little run and picking something to eat. When all the birds feeding on a winter marsh fly up, you may see a flock of birds keeping together and flying high up in chevron formation (like a broad inverted V). These will be Golden Plovers.

Both the Lapwing and the Golden Plover belong to the large family of birds called

" Waders." Waders have long legs and often
long bills, and most Waders are marsh or shore
birds. There they wade in the shallow water,
probing the sand or mud for worms, shrimps
and small animals on which they feed. But the
Lapwing, besides being called the Peewit because
of its call, is also called the Green Plover because
its back is really a beautiful green. So it is not
very strange that flocks of these two birds feed
together. Wading birds nest on the ground and
lay larger though fewer eggs in comparison to
the hedge and tree nest building birds. But the
young leave the nest very soon after they are dry
from the shell out of which they have come.
They are covered with down and have their eyes
open like little ducklings. The parents lead them
to where there is suitable food and the young
feed themselves, but the mother looks after them
and broods them at night. You may see the
downy young of the Lapwing in the cornfield in
April and May. They crouch and the mottled
colour of their down makes them difficult to see.
The parents will be swooping down and calling,
and it is kinder not to stay about too long then.
Young birds want food and they soon get chilled
if there is a cold wind blowing.

Plate 13   STARLING AT NEST HOLE

Plate 14   KESTREL WITH FIELD VOLE
                      (page 59)

CHAPTER 7

OWLS

MANY people think of Owls as birds of the night.
They connect them with old ruins, ghosts, and
weird sounds. The truth is that Owls are the
farmers' best friends in protecting laden barns
and stacks from the ravages of rats and mice.
Therefore we should delight when we hear
Owls at night, for then we know they are about,
searching out the vermin that eat our food.

We have five different kinds of Owls that are
quite common in this country. Two of them, the
Little Owl and the Short Eared Owl, regularly
hunt by day and you can watch them so doing.
The Barn Owl, or Screech Owl, is out hunting
on a winter afternoon and does not seem to mind
you watching him. The other two, the Long
Eared Owl and the Tawny Owl, do not usually
come out till it is nearly dark. The only way
one sees them well is if you are lucky enough to
find where they roost, hidden in the ivy growing
thickly on an old tree in the wood, or happen to
find their nests.

The Little Owl was brought over to this
country about seventy years ago. It has now
spread to nearly all counties of England and
many hard words have been said about this
Owl that were and are not true. Admittedly it

once was an alien, but it does far more good than harm if we believe the investigations that have been made about its habits and food. I see this Owl so often sitting in the hedgerow trees or flying over the corner of a field, it has become part of the bird life of the hedge for me which I should be sorry to lose. Often too I hear several calling harshly to each other. You should look out for this Little Owl whenever you are walking by the field paths along the hedge. Like all Owls it has a big head and a fluffy face. The two eyes look to the front and are not placed at the sides of the head as in so many birds. Then there is the strong, curved bill, like a nose. In fact many Owls' faces with their special surround of feathers, called the " facial disc," look like some human faces. When it flies it seems " bull-headed " though otherwise it is not much larger than a Blackbird. It is grey in colour and its wings are rounded. I have never seen a Little Owl fly across the middle of a field in daylight. It will cut off a corner but otherwise flies close to the hedge in low, bounding flight. To look at it perched on the tree it appears to have no neck, like a frog. Actually it has more neck than some other birds, but this is hidden by feathers. This is true of all the Owls, and you can prove it when you next find one perching close against the bole of a tree. Don't make any sudden movement, but just go quietly round the tree. You will find the Owl turns its head so that it is looking at you all the time till the head is nearly turned back to front.

The Barn Owl is another Owl of the farms. There is no missing him when he comes out of the barn loft in the twilight to fly in reeling flight round the stacks and across the stubble. He looks a great, light buff bird with rounded wings that are a yard across. He is the Owl that screeches and I know from experience that if one or a pair have their home among the rafters above your bedroom you will hear snores and hisses as well as some shrieks. But Barn Owls are better than cats for keeping the place clear from rats and mice. Indeed, they will catch several in a night and sometimes people have seen them sitting quietly with the tail of a rat hanging from their bill because the rat was too 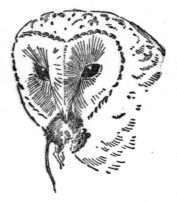 big a mouthful to swallow all at once. The Owl's flight is a silent flight. If you find an Owl's wing feather it is downy on both sides whereas in most birds the feathers have shiny under-sides. Thus, this Owl flies down the hedge-row or the ditch silently flapping his rounded wings. He reels this way and that, just a little above a tall hedge, searching through the dark-ness for any movement of an animal, and even spying one that is still. For all night-hunting Owls can see in the dark, because at the back of their eyes the cells of the retina are specialised

to see things in the dark that we should miss.
The Barn Owl sometimes takes small birds,
principally House Sparrows, that he finds roosting
in the ivy.

The Short Eared Owl is seen on the marshes,
hunting low over the reed beds, on desolate
moors and heaths, and even on wastelands and
sand-dunes by the sea. He is a big grey-brown
bird, slightly larger than the Barn Owl. He

hunts by day un-
less the sun is bright
and hot. He flies
low down, reeling
this way and that,
on large and slowly
beating wings. Then
he swoops down
and clutches a vole
with a foot. The
grasp is so powerful
that the life is squeezed out of the animal in a
moment. Two or three jabs with the strong
hooked bill and the vole is swallowed whole.
But you might well ask if the bird can digest
the fur and the bones. The Short Eared Owl
throws up these indigestible portions of the
meal as an egg-shaped pellet. You find these
pellets especially near the roost. If you carefully
examine them they tell you what the bird has
been eating by finding the bones, fur and feathers
of different animals and the wing-cases of insects.
All the Owls and Hawks bring up pellets of the
indigestible portions of the meal.

The bird is called the Short Eared Owl because it has two feathered tufts or horns on the top of its head. These have nothing to do with the bird's ears, which are two little holes covered with feathers behind the eyes.

The Tawny Owl is a bird which you will not see very often. It usually roosts by day and only comes out of its hiding-place to hunt by night. But if the country round you has plenty of small woods, hedgerow trees and parkland, then you will hear this Owl's call night after night. For me it has one of the most pleasing sounds of the country night. It is the Owl that calls " tu-whit, tu-whoo," although that is not what it says very often. The call is usually a long quavering " whoo." It is an oboe-like sound—that wood-wind instrument in the orchestra that has a glorious reedy note which you can always pick out when it plays. The call then is like an oboe player trying a tune on his own. You listen to it in the silence of the night and it will please you to hear it as much as it does me. I am often out at night and I hear it, and then lean against the gate leading into the field. I look against the night sky and sometimes I see a Tawny Owl go in wavering flight quickly down the hedge. Then I hear it calling again. You can hear the Tawny Owl call in the London parks at night.

CHAPTER 8

HAWKS

THERE are many different kinds of birds as well as Owls that live on meat. Eagles, Kites, Falcons and Hawks, Buzzards and Harriers, all live largely on the flesh of animals and birds that they seek out and capture. Because of this we should be careful not to think they are necessarily cruel birds. Many of us eat meat, and keep cats who kill mice and birds, to say nothing of the other thoughtless things we do.

All these birds of prey used to be very much more numerous up to a hundred and fifty years ago. There were not nearly so many people living in England then. Now where there are fields and hedges, in those days were often great forests and scrub-hills. In these Eagles and Kites had their homes. Kites with their long forked tails soared over London and other towns as well as the villages. Eagles and Falcons nested on the sea cliffs where now thousands of holiday-makers go for recreation. Gradually the large birds of prey were driven out from their own haunts and collecting eggs and stuffed birds became a craze. The rarer the bird became the more some persons sought to kill it. So you can see alterations in population, changes in farming methods, and changes in people's ideas have

effects on the birds around us. To-day there are
only a few Golden Eagles and a few Kites still
nesting in Britain, and their numbers can increase only if everyone takes more pleasure in
watching these magnificent birds than in running
for a gun to shoot them. Even then they would
never become very numerous in our densely
populated islands.

Our commonest Hawk now is the Kestrel.
It is the bird you see above the meadow, fanning
its wings and spreading or depressing its tail
so that it remains in the same position. A
Kestrel will remain stationary for several minutes
while it looks at the ground beneath, trying to
spot a mouse moving in the grass. If it does
it seems to slide down on the air, and grab it.
If nothing is to be seen, it makes a few sharp
wing beats and glides away to another field.
There again it fans, hovering in the air watching
and waiting. The bird is often called the " Wind-
hover " because of this habit. The Kestrel is
not just hanging and hovering in the air, but
it really is flying against the wind at a speed
equal to that of the wind so that the bird remains
stationary. You will see the Kestrel has to use
its tail more as a brake when the wind is gentle
than when there is a good breeze. Besides being
often seen over farm country, you will see
Kestrels by the shore, heaths, moors and marshes.
But always you can tell them by this hovering
habit of theirs. The tail is long and the wings
are pointed, and the female is brownish while
the male is chestnut in colour. The male also

has a slate-coloured head and tail except for a black band at its end. The female has dark stripes the whole length of the tail. Kestrels feed principally on mice and voles. Therefore we should do everything we can to protect these birds. They also take rats, moles and shrews. It is unfortunate about the shrew—those little mouse-like animals with a long nose like a beginning of a trunk—for it is a meat eater itself and lives on grubs in the soil, and so helps to rid the ground of pests. Of course, you must always remember shrews, as well as insect-eating birds, do not eat only injurious insects. They eat spiders and centipedes as well as caterpillars and wireworms, our friends and enemies alike. The Kestrel sometimes will take small birds if it is hungry and also grasshoppers and beetles. I have watched Kestrels hovering about the height of the telephone wires and dropping down again and again to the meadows when there were hundreds of " daddy-long-legs " on the grass.

You do not see a Sparrow Hawk nearly as often as you see a Kestrel. They are not so numerous, although there are plenty about in farm country and woodlands. But while the Kestrel hovers above the fields for all to see, the Sparrow Hawk dashes along the hedge first this side and then that. In a flash he is gone, and you may not see him again in the neighbourhood. He hunts the hedges and orchards where I live. He flies up the hedge, crosses over to the other side and chases a screaming Blackbird, that he has

Plate 15

SPARROW HAWK WITH NEST AND YOUNG

COMMON GULL WITH NEST AND EGGS

failed to grab in his strong claws, in and out of
the orchard trees and garden bushes until he has
caught it. Then the Sparrow Hawk flies to a flat
stump of a tree in the wood, or a clear place in
the meadow, to pluck and eat his capture. You
will see him make a " tent " by arching his wings
to touch the ground while he eats.

The Sparrow Hawk's method of hunting tells
you which bird it is as surely as the Kestrel's
hovering gives you the name of that bird. But
with the Sparrow Hawk the male and female
are different not only in the colour of their
plumage, but also in their size. The male has
a ruddy breast which is barred with darker lines
while the back is a slate-grey in colour. The
female is browner on the back and paler beneath,
nearly white, with brown bars. Both birds have
much shorter and more rounded wings than the
Kestrel but a longer tail. In many Hawks the
female is larger and a more powerful bird than
the male. And that is so with the Sparrow Hawks.
though with the Kestrel there is not much
difference between the sexes.

In the west country, Devon combes and Welsh
valleys, Exmoor, the Pennines and the Lake
District, a much larger bird of prey is seen soaring
round and round. All the time they go, for
there are usually two, higher and higher with
their wings spread out and the end feathers
separated like fingers. Sometimes they go so
high, soaring, that they become mere specks
against a white cloud. They do not seem to
be using their wings, except by keeping them

outstretched they are able to sail round and round, using the air currents and the wind—in fact they are gliding. These dark-brown birds are Buzzards —the Common Buzzard. They are lovely birds to watch and they do a lot of good by catching voles, moles and rabbits. Luckily for the Buzzards, and those of us who enjoy watching them, there is not so much game preserving of Pheasants, Partridges and Grouse as there were fifty years ago. Then gamekeepers shot all Hawks and Owls they saw and trapped them by setting traps on poles on which Hawks often perch. It was a cruel way of killing Hawks and now it has been made illegal to set traps in this way. Like many cruel things it was stupid, too, to kill the birds who were keeping down rats and mice. Buzzards make big nests, sometimes on the ground amongst the heather of the moor, in a tree and sometimes on a cliff. The young, like the other birds of prey, become covered with down before they get their feathers.

Plate 17   KINGFISHER

CHAPTER 9

BIRDS OF THE WATERSIDE

THERE are lots of birds that live by the water. Some, like the Coot and Grebe, spend most of their time on it. All these birds live by the water because they find the food they like to eat there. Some are fish eaters. Others are vegetarians and eat water weeds. How can we tell which is which? If the bird has a dagger-like bill he probably uses it for fish and not for vegetables. Have you seen a Kingfisher? He comes flying along the stream, a brilliant blue bird flashing in and out of the sunbeams and shade of the alder bushes growing on the bank. He is so quick that you should suspect he has to catch something for his living. Then when he perches on a branch over-hanging the water and you see his strong dagger bill you know he is after fish and not water weed. His feet are bright red and his breast is a ruddy chestnut colour. But you have hardly time to see this before he seems to drop with a splash into the stream beneath. Up he comes again at once with a fish in his bill, settles on his perch while the shining drops of water roll off his lovely feathers. The Kingfisher also eats fresh-water shrimps and other animals harmful to fish. Thus Kingfishers are good birds to have on a trout stream although they may catch some trout.

A Heron, too, has a long sharp bill and he has long legs as well. He catches fish, but in a different way from the Kingfisher. Instead of being a little bird like the Kingfisher a Heron is probably the largest wild bird most of us ever see. You see a Heron flying high above the water, his great rounded wings flapping slowly. His long neck is folded so that the head seems to come out from the shoulders. But the legs are carried straight and can be seen projecting beyond the tail. He glides down nearer and nearer. One more sweep of his wings to lift him over a fringe of reeds, and he lowers his legs gently into the water. There is no splash, no noise. He stands still for a few minutes and then strides through the shallows, his long neck strained forward, his eyes peering into the water. Suddenly he stabs with his bill right below the surface and brings a squirming eel into the air. Sometimes he pierces a frog, at other times a fish, with his bill. A Heron will stand in the water, motionless, waiting for a fish to swim near. The eyes of a Heron must be very sharp and the bird must keep them open under water to see his prey, so he does not have to allow for the refraction (an object in water is not where it seems to us on the bank). Water voles, mice, and birds and their eggs are also eaten by Herons.

If the Heron is full grown you cannot help noticing his long crest feathers. Young ones have hardly any crest when you see them first on the marsh in late June, looking rather like

Plate 18

HERONS

bewildered new boys. And well they might because they have just flown from the nest in a clump of tall trees where their parents reared them in company with several other pairs of Herons. These nesting sites of Herons are called heronries and you see the great nests of sticks like small platforms. Some old naturalists tried to teach people that Herons made holes to put their legs through when sitting on their eggs. That shows how careful you should be in your observations and write down nothing that you have not seen yourself and believe to be true.

So we have now two very different looking birds who live on fish but catch them in different ways. There are other kinds of birds that catch fish by chasing them under the water. The Great Crested Grebe is a common bird of lakes and reservoirs. You see a pair leisurely swimming on the water. Every now and then one dives and is under the water from ten to twenty seconds. The bird reappears sometimes quite a distance away. It has been swimming under water and getting a small fish or other under-water insect or animal and may also take some water weeds to eat. This Grebe is about the size of a farmyard duck, but it has a different shape. Its body is long and it swims low in the water, in fact it will swim with its back awash or even so low that only its head and neck show. The Grebe has little tail and so its shape in the water is that of a submarine. This likeness impresses one all the more when, as often happens, the bird lets itself sink down instead of diving head

5

when the apples are ripe in the orchards the Moorhens will go there from the lake and feed on fallen fruit. Some say that they will climb trees to get the fruit. I have no doubt they could, but I have never seen them do it, perhaps because there have been always hundreds of fallen apples under the trees. When you walk towards them they walk away from you. Quicker and quicker they go, the wings flap and they manage to get "airborne." Their long legs trail beneath them, brushing the reed tops and the water. They swim now and hide themselves in the reeds and if necessary they sink their whole body in the water, leaving only their red bill showing, till they think the danger has passed.

Their nest with eight or nine eggs is easy to find on the river and pond bank. If you do not disturb them you will very likely see the black downy young with brilliant coloured heads.

Swans and Geese have stout legs and their three toes are joined together with a membrane which we call a "web." Ducks have a similar type of legs and feet. They are smaller birds and most of us see many more Ducks than ever we do Swans and Geese. There are many kinds of Ducks, some of them are found on fresh water, others like the Eider Duck are sea birds. Again some Ducks, like the farmyard Ducks and the Mallard, which is their wild relation, paddle about and up-end when they see something to eat below the surface. Others, like the little black-and-white Tufted Duck which you see

MOORHEN AND YOUNG

Plate 19

on lakes in the parks, very often dive right under when feeding. Most Ducks have a blunt, broad bill with which they sift and shovel the silt and weeds they find round the water and in marsh pools. You have probably seen Ducks doing this and so getting seeds, weeds, and minute snails, insects, and other animals on which they feed. And the webs joining their toes makes it easier for these birds to walk on soft ground without sinking in and getting bogged. When I was very young someone told me that Ducks were able to swim because they had webbed feet. Actually, the webbed feet help them to walk. The Moorhen and Heron have toes without either webs or lobes, but both these birds can swim. The Grebe and the Coot have extra " skin " on their toes, but not webs joining one on to the other. Divers, who are near relations to the Grebes, have not only webbed feet, but in these birds the toe which is usually at the back of the foot is turned to the front and connected with the other three toes by the web.

CHAPTER 10

SEA GULLS

EVERYONE needs a holiday if they are to work well, and when you are young you should have more than one holiday a year. The seaside is the place for these. If you have been to the seaside in the summer and also in the winter you should have noticed that there were many more Sea Gulls on the shore in winter. For in winter tens of thousands of Gulls have come from the north and east to crowd our shores and estuaries, rivers, lakes and reservoirs, our fields and valleys. They are here because they can find food in abundance. You see them gliding on the storm winds, or flying with slow beats of their angled wings, all the time searching the water. Now and then they dip down, unfold their legs in case they want to steady themselves on the water, and seize some floating garbage. Often, too, you will see hundreds of Gulls standing on the shore together doing nothing but resting while they wait for the tide to go out when they can find worms, crabs, shell-fish and other stranded fish and animals. Take this opportunity to try and pick out the different kinds of Gulls.

At first it seems very difficult to distinguish the various Gulls, but it is not really, once you know there are only five kinds that you commonly see on the beach, and there is another one, the Kittiwake, that keeps well out to sea usually. First you eliminate all brown-plumaged birds, or those with a black band at the end of their tail : for all these are young birds and you can learn their different plumages after you can tell at a glance the five common kinds of Gulls in adult plumage. Three of our Gulls are large birds. They are the Great Black Backed Gull, the Lesser Black Backed Gull, and the Herring Gull. We have one medium-sized Gull called the Common Gull, and a small Gull that we know as the Black Headed Gull though all the winter it has a white head. In the flock of full-sized Gulls standing together on the beach most of them have grey backs except for a little black and white where the tips of the wings are folded over the tail. These are Herring Gulls. They have pink legs and feet and a big yellow bill with a red spot on it. Then there are some Gulls with black backs and white heads that are even bigger than the Herring Gulls. These are Great Black Backed Gulls, our largest and fiercest Gull. They also have pink legs and yellow bill with a red spot. There may be a Gull with a back which is neither wholly black nor grey. He is probably a Lesser Black Backed Gull, but you can make sure if you see his legs are yellow. Why you may not see many Lesser Black Backed Gulls in the depth of winter is because most of them go farther south than this country as autumn turns to winter. When flying all three of these large, Gulls show black wing tips with white spots, which are called " mirrors." Some of them have white at the very tip of the wings.

The large Gulls keep more to the shore than the smaller Gulls, although the Herring Gull is often seen inland. Some people think these Gulls uninteresting, just seeing them standing there doing apparently nothing. But watch ! There is a Herring Gull marking time on the sand with his webbed feet till he has made a little quicksand, and now he can get worms and shrimps and other creatures for his tea. Another Gull has found a mussel. Up he flies with it and drops it on the shingle. So that is the way he opens his mussels and winkles. Sometimes though I have seen a gull repeatedly but ineffectively drop mussels on the wet sands. Any wounded bird or sickly sheep is soon devoured by the large Gulls. On the east coast they gather in swarms in the autumn when the herring drifters have shot their miles of nets. And when the nets are being hauled the Gulls, from a distance, hide the boats as though in swirling snow as they scramble for the silver fish that drop from the net. I have spent many nights with Gulls in their breeding colonies and seen and heard them greet the dawn sun with their loud, laughing cries. I find it difficult to distinguish the calls of the different Gulls, but if you have a good ear it is possible.

The Common Gull is medium sized, with a grey back like the Herring Gull. It has greenish legs and bill, and the bill itself is finer and has no red spot as the larger Gulls have. Although you often see Common Gulls on the shore, they feed on the fields and meadows near the coast during the winter. With them on the fields you will also see the Black Headed Gulls. These are a smaller Gull, especially noticeable is its smaller head. At this season of the year the Black Headed Gulls have two dark spots on each side of their otherwise white head. The Common Gulls have neat, faintly streaked heads. The Black Headed have red legs and bill. The place to see Black Headed Gulls is the Thames Embankment, if you are in London in the winter. And they are by rivers in other towns, and also are often seen being fed from the promenades of segside towns. They come in the autumn and go at the end of March. By that time you will see many of them getting their " black " heads. If you are close enough you will find this so-called black is a lovely chocolate brown. These brown feathers have been there all the winter but were hidden because the feathers had white tips. Only when the tips have been worn down by wear and tear of winter use do the neat chocolate heads show. That often happens with birds ; their smart wedding-dress is one that they have worn all the winter.

As the winter passes, the majority of Gulls leave the shores and the towns where they have spent the winter, and go to their nesting haunts. All these five Gulls nest in colonies. The Black Headed Gull nests in colonies, sometimes in the shore, sometimes on islands of inland lakes. I have seen them on Scoulton Mere in Norfolk, where nearly ten thousand pairs nest every year

on a small island nearly forty miles from the sea.
And there are some colonies larger than this one
and many more smaller. The other gulls do not
have such large colonies as this Gull nor do they
go inland, though sometimes the Common Gull
does. Some Gulls make a large nest of seaweed,
heather, reeds, or whatever is handy on the
ground. But the Herring and the Black Backed
Gulls often nest on ledges of cliffs or rocks.
Many of the larger gulls go to the north or east
away from this country to breed

BLACK HEADED GULL

CHAPTER II

FINCHES ON THE FARM

FARMS are the most important places in the world. Without them we should starve, for on them our food is produced. We want more and better farms everywhere because about half the people of the world have not enough to eat. A very great man on these things, Lord Boyd Orr, has said that we must double the amount of food we produce in the world in a generation. If we fail there will be a world disaster. On the other hand an eminent American says that as there is not enough food to go round it is better for America not to sell food abroad. Then the people in other countries would die out except those that could be fed from food produced on the farms of each country.

That shows you how important farms are to-day. And wherever there are farms there are birds. If the crops grown on a farm are changed, or the cultivation is altered, then there is a corresponding change among the birds there. If the hedges are uprooted in order to make larger fields, many of the birds will go. Because many of the farm birds nest in the hedges, and the number of birds in a given area is regulated by the simple fact of the number of nesting sites in the neighbourhood. In this the birds are like us : they cannot live and work where there are no houses or places to build them. If the farm is not properly looked after and cultivation is neglected, thistles will become abundant. So flocks of Goldfinches will come to feed upon the thistle down, or rather the seeds at the base of the down. The birds hang on to the thistle stems rather like Blue Tits on hedge twigs. The stem bends with their weight till the Goldfinches are upside-down picking out the seeds. Sometimes they will hover over a thistle head while getting the seed. It is then, and at any time when Goldfinches fly, you see the broad wing bands of brilliant yellow from which they get their name. They are a slender Finch and not only have they brightly coloured wings but they also have scarlet faces, white cheeks and a black cap. Young Goldfinches when they are about during their first summer have not coloured faces, though you cannot mistake them because they have the golden wings like their parents. I know villages on the edge of wastelands where Goldfinches are so numerous that you see them constantly in the gardens and even by the side of the road.

Finches are seed-eating birds and naturally many of them are attracted by the grain that is grown for us on farms. But there are many kinds of Finches and they do not eat corn all the time. They are hard-, stout-billed birds and many of them eat great quantities of weed seeds, as we know the Goldfinches do. Thus the autumn stubbles attract Finches and we find them flocking to the stackyards during the winter. If we want to see all the Finches in the neighbourhood, the time for that is the day after the corn stack has been threshed. Weed seeds and tail corn litter the ground and flocks of Finches are there for this feast. There will be the Chaffinch, walking perkily about, looking neat, with bold white shoulder patches. The cocks are pinkish chestnut on the breast and have a slate-blue head. The hens are a sober olive-brown, but the white shoulders make it impossible to mistake her for any other bird. There will be plenty of House Sparrows and perhaps a pair or more of the smaller, brown-capped, white-checked Tree Sparrows. These latter are never very plentiful and should be protected as they do more good than harm. There are a pair of birds with a shade of green in their plumage and a yellow streak on the wings. They are Greenfinches. Their bills are stouter than a Sparrow's and they are a slightly larger bird. The cocks are much greener than the hens. There is a yellowish bird, perhaps several, which are about the same size as the House Sparrows. That is a Yellow Hammer, or Yellow Bunting. A pair will nest in the hedge bottom and take dust baths in the fine tilth of newly sown fields when the chestnut tree is white with spikes of blossoms next May. Sometimes there will be some birds like large Hen Sparrows, with brown, streaked plumage. This is a flock of Corn Buntings. Like the Tree Sparrows we do not find them on every farm.

CHAPTER 12

BIRDS OF COMMONS AND DOWNS

In England to-day fewer people in proportion to our population grow food than in any other country of the world. It was different two hundred years ago. Then what ground was cultivated was mostly done by the villagers in common fields in which each household cultivated several strips. The common was very important then because there the cattle used to graze. Trees and woods on part of the common land provided the villagers with timber to build their huts and fuel to warm them in winter.

Then the industrial epoch began. Crops were grown now to sell to the townspeople, and not only to feed the villagers as in the past had been the main motive. Farming became an industry. Landowners enclosed the common land, sometimes without paying for it. The many village peasants, having lost their land, went to work in mines and town factories. Although this caused hardship to country people the new methods greatly increased the amount of food the land produced. Without this increase the industrial revolution would have been delayed and the population could not have increased.

So you see why we have so few commons now and why they are on poor sandy soil that would

not pay to farm. But there are many birds that like these gorse-covered commons, these wind-swept curving downlands, and the wastelands by the sea—the Stonechat, the Whinchat, the Wheat-ear, the Linnet, the Meadow Pipit and the Lark.

The Stonechat is a bird about the size and shape of a Robin. He perches on a spray at the top of a gorse bush, a showy little bird with his black head, white collar and shoulder patch on the lovely brown plumage. The hen has not the black head and white collar, but you know her by the constant movement of the tail and flicking of the wings that Stonechats are always doing when perched on a bush or a fence. They are near relatives to our Robin. When the young first fly they are more like the young Robins, having a mottled plumage. Stonechats also are continually calling their name, " chat, chat," or something near it. You may see a bird very similar to the hen Stonechat, and acting like a Stonechat too, but it is not quite so plump and this bird has a distinct white eye-stripe like an eyebrow. This is a Whinchat and at all ages you can see the eye-stripe though it is only in the cock that it is white. Some Stone-chats stay here all the winter, especially on wastelands by the coast, but Whinchats go in early autumn to winter in tropical Africa. In September you might mistake them for a Warbler, because they are rather a slender kind of bird, if you do not note what a short tail they have. Both these birds feed much on the ground.

Another bird near to the Robin family is the

6

from the rough grass. You can see he is a brown streaky bird with quite a long tail which has white outer feathers, but the head feathers are raised in a little crest as he sings ; for he begins to sing when he still is near the ground. Up he flies, climbing on fluttering wings till he is a speck against the sunlit blue sky. And all the time his song comes cascading down. He sweeps round a little and then in a wider sweep he begins slowly to descend. His song ends only when he is near the ground. Then his wings close and he dives into the grass, runs a little way and is soon hidden. He does not go to the nest—in fact Skylarks sing in winter before the nest is built. Even the hen will not go directly to the nest, which is built of grass and rootlets in a depression in the ground. Skylarks have a long straight hind claw, and they, too, like the Pipits, are near relatives to the Wagtails.

On the gorse bush, singing a pleasant song, half twittering and half twanging, is a little brown bird with crimson feathers on his breast and head. That is a Linnet. Linnets like commons and bushy wasteland, but you get them on the farm too, and I sometimes have a nest in my garden. They go where they can find small seeds, for they are Finches. The hen has no crimson feathers, but you cannot mistake Linnets for any other bird of the common because they are much browner birds. When they are flying they keep up a quick, constant twittering. In the winter, Linnets flock together and feed on the stubble fields.

H. Marcus Stone

Plate 21 GOLDFINCH WITH NEST AND YOUNG (*page* 76)

CHAPTER 13

SOMETHING MORE ABOUT BIRDS

IN the chapters of this book I have told you something about the birds you are likely to see in various surroundings and about some bird families. Not in any way have I tried to give you a full description of any bird, but I have given you hints to help you to identify some of our common birds. To be able to name a bird quickly is a great encouragement. Yet do not let that prevent you from making full notes about it. If you really want to become a good bird watcher and get true amusement out of it, you must build up good notes and be constantly adding to them.

There are many bird books in which you can look up a full description of the birds you have seen. In your local library you should be able to look at the five volumes of *The Handbook of British Birds*. There you will find a coloured plate of any bird that has ever been found in Britain, the cock, hen and the young, and all of them in spring and winter plumage. Besides that, there is a concise description of everything at present known about the bird. Next to this there is the late T. A. Coward's *Birds of the British Isles and their Eggs*. This is a small two-volume work by a man who devoted his life to bird watching and wrote from the vast store of his notes, and you will find it an enormous help. These two volumes have coloured plates of all our common birds. *Watching Birds*, by James Fisher—a " Pelican " book—is the most interesting book about birds in general that I know. It tells you, amongst other things, what they are and what they do. It tells you that there are about 120 million birds in Britain altogether, about their territories, courtship and migration, and also how you can study them. As you learn more about birds, the more useful you will find the book.

Have you ever thought how different we are from birds ? It really isn't a great wonder when you know that man evolved from the apes while birds evolved from the lizards. Work and the use of his hands had a great deal to do with man's rise from the apes. The need for explaining to others how to use his hands led to speech. The speech centre of our brain is next to that of the centre for the right hand, in a right-handed man. But the birds evolved from the lizards who climbed trees to escape from their enemies. Gradually, the scales with which the lizards were covered became feathers although, with few exceptions, the legs and feet remained scaly. They developed long feathers on their fore-limbs and enormous chests to house the great central keel bone and thick muscles strong enough to work their wings for flying. If man had wings he would probably have to develop a chest a yard thick to house the muscles needed to fly a little way.

But not all birds can fly. The Ostrich runs or walks; the Penguins swim and walk; the Ducks can fly, swim and walk; Swifts can progress only by flying. Yet it is the wings that we think of as characteristic of birds. A bird's wing is its fore-limb. The first bone of the wing is similar to the first bone in our arms—the one where our biceps show. Then comes the two-boned forearm. Beyond that are the wrist, fingers and thumb. The index, or first, finger has the long feathers springing from it. The thumb and third finger are very small and are called the " bastard wing " which you find with a few feathers at the end of the wing. The long feathers are called " primaries "; the shorter ones that come from the forearm are called " secondaries." There are three other layers of feathers covering the wings. The outer layer, nearest the wing's edge, is called " greater wing coverts," the next, the " medium," and, next the body, the " lesser wing coverts." The shorter feathers covering the shafts of the long tail feathers are known as " tail coverts." These spring from the tail end of the rump of the bird.

The eyesight of a bird is very sharp. It has to be, not only to give warning of danger but also for seeing its food. Therefore its eyes and their sockets take up a lot of room in a bird's skull. A bird can hear, but its external ear is a small hole, hidden under the head feathers, behind and below the eye. Birds have only a poor sense of smell. They have no teeth. Their food is wetted with saliva (which helps its digestion),

swallowed into the gullet, and is squeezed into
the stomach where it is ground up and begins
to be digested. In some birds the gullet has
a muscular sac called the " crop." Birds are
warm-blooded creatures. They have a heart
that pumps the blood round their bodies after the
red corpuscles of it have taken up a fresh supply
of oxygen from the lungs. The female, or hen
bird, produces eggs. These develop in the ovary.
Birds have only one ovary that produces eggs.
When an egg is ripe it receives a cell, called a
sperm, from the male. Then the egg becomes coated
with albumen, or the "white of an egg," in the pass-
age called the oviduct, and lastly with the porous
chalky shell. At last, having travelled down the
oviduct into the cloaca, it is laid blunt end first
in the nest. The male bird injects many sperms
into the hen when he " treads " her in pairing.
There are two different kinds of egg cells in
each female bird, one of which will produce a
male and the other a female young. A male bird
produces only one kind of sperm cell. In
mammals it is just the opposite, for here the male
produces two kinds of sperm cells and the female
only one kind of egg cell. In birds the number
of eggs laid varies with the different kinds of
birds. The Gannets usually lay only one egg,
but Partridges may lay as many as twenty. The
domestic chicken will lay two or three hundred
eggs a year, but that is because they have been
scientifically bred for laying. Another thing is
that if there is no male bird to pair with the
female she will nevertheless lay eggs, and even

sit on them, but they never hatch because they have not got the male cell in them. It is the male and female cell joining together and then dividing into millions of cells which at last makes the young living chick.

The wastage among wild birds is enormous. If a pair of birds live five years (and some live longer) they only produce on an average two of their kind that grow up and breed during the whole of the five years of their lives. If it were not so, and a pair produced two more that bred next year and went on like that for five years, you would have a terrific increase in the numbers of birds, which would have serious consequences. Nevertheless it is a warning to us to do everything we can to guard nests and eggs. The birds have quite enough natural enemies without us adding to their number. My advice is not to collect eggs. They become a nuisance. They teach you nothing, and at last you become ashamed of them. Watch the nest, take notes, and you will have something that you will always be proud of. It is in the spring, in the nesting season, that the birds sing. You should listen for their songs, learn to know them so that you can tell what bird is singing, and at what date. Notice, too, when each stops to sing, and what difference there is in the summer and autumn song. Try and find out what singing has to do with taking up a special area of ground in the nesting season into which a male bird will not allow another bird of his kind except his mate. For songs are more often warnings to other birds to " keep off " than love songs. After the nesting season many pairs of birds flock and live together till next spring. Others, like Rooks, are in flocks all the year round.

Most birds migrate. Some do not even leave the country but they go from their nesting areas southward in hard weather. Others go to France and Spain, and many go as far south as the equator and farther. Birds are often caught by head winds, fog and snow. Then their disasters not only tell us of the hazardous nature of migration but also of its immensity. During one wintry spell one autumn in America it was estimated that no fewer than three-quarters of a million Lapland Buntings lay dead on the ice of two small lakes in Minnesota. Not only that, but similar reports came in from observers over 1500 square miles. Anyone who has watched the immense number of birds migrating from this country in the autumn realises the return migration in the spring is but a trickle compared to those that went. Birds have a power of orientation, or place finding, but it is by no means " fool proof." Even with Homing Pigeons, especially bred for this, only about five per cent. survive to race over long distances. Many theories have been put out in trying to explain how it is migrant birds are able to find their way back over often thousands of miles to nest again in the same stable, field, garden or wood. But up to the present all these theories have been proved incorrect. Whatever sense may guide birds on most of their journey, it is thought that they do recognise landmarks in territory familiar to them.

The problem is to explain how birds navigate and find their way on long sea journeys when they are out of sight of land for hundreds of miles. For instance, New Zealand migrants must make a sea crossing of up to 900 miles and yet strike the land where it is their custom to.   The Ruby Throated Humming Bird crosses 500 miles of the Gulf of Mexico.   The American Golden Plover in the autumn flies from the Arctic, through Labrador, and crosses 2400 miles of the Atlantic to winter in Argentina.   In the spring it returns by a more westerly land route.   Some of the flocks of Geese that winter on our west coast estuaries come in by an easterly route and return via a more northerly route in the spring.   The Goldcrest, a bird weighing half an ounce, comes to us in autumn over the North Sea, a distance of 300 miles before they strike the Norfolk sand dunes, utterly fatigued.

Young Cuckoos migrate in autumn to Central and South Africa although their parents left this country before some of them were hatched from the egg.   Some birds migrate at night.   Some, like the Plovers, call continuously.   Others, like the Crows, migrate without uttering a sound.   Sometimes the young migrate on their own.   In the spring the males of many species come before the females.   Immature birds will migrate with adults.

Why should birds migrate ?   The reason is probably to go to a place which is most suitable for their young.   Many creatures who have changed their habits return to where they used to live in the distant past in order to breed. Seals come to dry land, frogs and newts to the water, salmon return to the rivers, eels return to the sea, and there are many other examples. The climate of our earth has changed. Most of Britain has more than once been covered with ice. It has also been as hot as the tropics now are. Birds have had to adapt themselves, but their young must be cared for under conditions of the past. Another thing is that there is only a twelve-hour day, roughly, near the equator. When the majority of birds are feeding young they want much more daylight to catch insects or fish.

Those of our migrants that winter in South Africa, and other places south of the equator, arrive there when it is spring or early summer. They will be amongst native birds busy in their nesting season. But our migrants will not nest again till they have returned to the north. This phenomenon of having some species of birds coming here for the summer but not breeding, while other species do, is something we do not find in this country. When our migrants arrive in Africa their reproductive glands have become small and inactive. It will not be till these are enlarging again that they begin their migration northward. Some southern hemisphere birds migrate northward, but not north of the equator. And some birds of the tropics, too, migrate. But the great land masses are in the northern hemisphere. And that there

GREENFINCH AT NEST (*page 77*)

Plate 23

Plate 24   BULLFINCH WITH NEST AND YOUNG (page 78)

should be good nesting sites more than anything else regulates the number of birds in an area, whether that area is a field or a hemisphere.

We are fortunate in Britain as regards studying migration. For most birds like to migrate along the coast. And we get great flocks of migrants coming from Greenland and Iceland, and Norway and the Baltic countries, streaming down our west and east coasts, and along the English Channel coast. Our scientists are now studying migration, and one of the things they have to do is to ring migrants. Thus, many birds have small leg rings put on them as nestlings, or when they are caught in special traps so as not to harm them. All these rings are numbered and if you find a dead bird please look and see if there is one of these small rings on its legs. If so, remove it and send it to the " British Museum, Bird Department, London," saying where and when you found it. In this way you will be helping to build up our knowledge of migration.

Above all, guard our wild birds, our flowers and our few native animals. Learn about them by watching them whenever you can. Try to understand the country folk whose skill and hard work do so much to make our country the beautiful land it is. If you find pleasure in these things, try to interest others. Join a local nature club, or society, and do some practical work with them.

I cannot end this small book better than by quoting from one of our best practical bird watchers, James Fisher : " To sum up ; for the rest of this century the British naturalists are going to be increasingly out of doors enjoying and assessing the wealth of British birds and other living things. The British countryside, less exploited, more loved and cared for, will be their playground. For the study of birds is play ; a science often, an art sometimes, but still play. And who shall stop the British at their honest play ? "

SKYLARK